Tyler is a young lady with multiple disabilities and has faced a lot of scrutiny for following her dreams and faced many people who didn't believe in her. Despite all the obstacles in life, Tyler is fierce and determined, and will not be defeated by anything or anyone who think she not capable of the things she wants.

Tyler aims to encourage more young people like herself to be braver and fiercer and to go against all odds when they come against them.

Tyler aims for the government to step in and make the workplace more inclusive to those with disabilities, without companies just ticking a box in their recruitment process or in their staffing levels. Tyler wants to see more disabled or those with disabilities in management positions, and more training in the workplace about how to work with those with disabilities – whether that be understanding how their mind works or learning BSL – whatever training may be offered. Tyler wants more understanding amongst colleagues, not criticism.

This book is dedicated to anyone who has felt like an outcast in society, whether that be because of other's treatment or their disabilities. I hope you all find the inner strength to break down barriers and re-define your own odds and accomplish all your dreams and goals in life.

I want to thank Austin Macauley for publishing the book. Without yourselves the book wouldn't be available for the world to see. You have given me an opportunity to educate society.

Tyler Casey

DISABILITY & ME

AUSTIN MACAULEY PUBLISHERS™

LONDON • CAMBRIDGE • NEW YORK • SHARJAH

A CIP catalogue record for this title is available from the British Library.

ISBN 9781035812684 (Paperback)
ISBN 9781035841592 (Hardback)
ISBN 9781035812691 (ePub e-book)

www.austinmacauley.com

First Published 2023
Austin Macauley Publishers Ltd®
1 Canada Square
Canary Wharf
London
E14 5AA

I'd like to thank my family – grandmother, brothers and sister, and friends. Special thanks to my mum for fighting my corner when I didn't myself and teaching me work ethic. My dad and my stepmother Marie for always being on the other side of the phone to listen to my cares and complains and supporting me through them. My nanny and Granda Bob for looking out for me and treating me just like their own – always. My best friend Georgia for being the best friend and god mother to my girl, and always being by our side in all we do.

And finally, my beautiful baby girl for not only teaching me how to be a mother but how to be the woman I am today. You gave me the strength and determination to want to help make the world a better place for you and others and I don't want history to repeat itself.

Table of Contents

Forward
Your Silence Is Deafening

Sorry, what's that... I can't hear you?

Oh... I see... you want to put me into that box, with that label, put me in that corner and then shuffle me down that non-descript path.

Please listen carefully... I will overfill every box you put me in and I will shout louder than anyone to make sure my story is heard even by those with the acutest case of selective hearing.

I am Tyler. I am passionate, driven, happy go lucky, friendly, a loving and caring mum, accountant, daughter, sister, friend and colleague.

If you have ever felt like society has put you in a box only to leave you there because they don't know what else to do with you, this is the book for you.

Equally, if, like a jack in the box, you have bounced straight back out of the box determined to go on your merry way down your (very own) path to success and happiness, then... hi, I just might be your girl! Very pleased to meet you!

To put it simply... I will not be put in a box, nor will I stand by anymore while someone else is!

Sorry... am I shouting? I have a tendency to do that – always have since I was a toddler.

I have a disability, you see. You can't see it but it's very real, very diagnosed, very life changing and very there all the time.

Sometimes I wish you could see it, maybe then I wouldn't have had to put up with the grief I have faced in my life.

I am partially deaf. I have dyslexia and dyscalculia. I have had more ear infections than I could count, more hospital visits than my fair share and more drops, pills, consultancies and painful blows to my heart than I would wish on anyone.

I am only 26 but already I am tired of my story falling on deaf ears, so I am using the power of the written word to shout it from the rooftops.

It's time for the discriminators and the bullies to listen and learn and it is time for other young disabled people to stand up proud and feel inspired to move a step closer to their very own happy ever after.

If my story can stop one more office, playground, classroom, corridor or zoom call turning into a toxic wasteland of hate and abuse then it will have been well worth the telling.

Any sort of disability in my opinion is just a label, a sticker that has been given to you by professionals. A creation formulated from an opinion. These professionals have got facts, degrees and educated reasons for giving you this diagnosis, yes, but their label is not the be all and end all. It does not need to define you, just because someone has told you that you have a disability that's not who you are, you can still change your life and carve out your own path.

My hope is that you will read my story and feel brave enough to go and carve out your own life, with your unique stamp all over it.

1. Twirling and Picnics

'Deaf people, we've simply got ears that don't work, that's it. We're not different in any other way it's just how we communicate.' Jo Rose is an Outreach Worker at Signal and a Deaf British Sign Language (BSL)

I am three. I love twirling. I love teddies. I love wellies. I love fields I love life.

I am twirling and twirling, faster and faster in my very own. I clutch my favourite teddy, Louise the Lamb. I laugh as I spin and everything becomes a whirl of colour, mostly greens, apart from the red patch of the tractor and the tiny little dot of my mum's bright yellow wellies in the distance.

I stop spinning and I am so dizzy, I fall onto the wet grass and look up at the sky which is a swirling mass of fluffy clouds.

I can feel the wet grass tickling the inside of my ears and its coolness is nice against my hot cheeks.

I climb up onto my wellied feet and race across the field towards the yard.

I spot my mum standing at the back of the Land Rover with her arms crossed. She looks a bit cross.

"Mum! Mum! Where's Jake? I want him to play with me and Louise the lamb!"

Mummy's face is level with mine, and she doesn't look happy.

"Tyler, stop yelling! I am right here! You don't need to be so loud? I have been calling you for the last half an hour. Why did you not answer?"

"I didn't hear you, Mummy. I promise. I was twirling so all the noise was maybe spinning, too."

"I was worried. I was calling and calling you and I couldn't see you anywhere."

"I was lying on the grass, Mummy, maybe that's why you couldn't see me, and the grass was in my ears so maybe that's why I didn't hear you."

"Well one thing's for sure, Tyler, when you go to school, you will have to listen much better than you do now!"

"I will listen super well in school, Mummy, I promise."

"Tyler, there you go again. Yelling at me! Shhhhh! I am RIGHT HERE!"

When I was three and twirling in fields, Mum didn't realise I had a disability. From the moment I could communicate at all, I was loud. My mum never thought anything of it because we were a loud family. We lived in the countryside and spent half our lives outdoors around noisy animals or machinery. We were always shouting above some sort of noise or to each other across a huge field or yard.

I was always a good bit louder than any of the others, which everyone else noticed except me. I didn't think I was loud. If anything, I thought everyone, including myself, was a little too quiet.

It wasn't until I was at primary school that my teachers noticed how difficult it was to get my attention with their voice alone. It got to the stage where they had to touch me on the shoulder and point at the board or stand right in front of me until I noticed them and then speak solely to me. Even then I was oblivious to just how different I was to all of my friends. My lovely Head Teacher, Mrs Sutton, spoke with my mum regularly about my lack of listening skills and together they concluded that it wasn't just a case of selective hearing. My mum had so much respect for Mrs Sutton that, as soon as she sensed her concern, she made an ENT appointment for me to get a hearing test.

I remember that test so well because the experience was so much fun. I was about six or seven years old. They gave me headphones and a little button to press as and when I heard the sound. I remember turning to my mum and delightfully declaring, mum I look like a weathergirl.

After the hearing test, we saw the ENT consultant who informed us of something shocking. I was partially deaf. I was fully deaf in my right ear and had only a percentage of hearing in my left ear. I was told I would have to wear hearing aids.

Despite being seated in a huge chair in the very formal setting of the grey-haired old school consultant's office as he told me that I was deaf and would have to wear a hearing aid, I was delighted.

How exciting! A hearing aid! I would have something the other children wouldn't have. I wondered… What will it look like? How does it work? What will everything sound like now … ?

I simply couldn't wait to get my hands on it and play with it, I guess.

Sadly, there was more news to come that would really impact my mum. The ENT consultant went on to inform us that I was born deaf and that it was on my hospital records. Somehow my mother had never been informed.

I looked at my mum sitting behind me in that office and delight was the last emotion she was feeling. Looking back now, she looked like a whole dolly mixture of shame, frustration, shock and sadness.

It was then my mum left the room for a short time to process this news.

2. Free to Be Me

A child's hearing loss is so critical for development. Even partial hearing loss can result in an impaired ability to speak and acquire language.

– Alison Cassady

On the same day as my diagnosis, I had a silicone mould taken of my ear to make my very own bespoke hearing aid.

For the next few days, I was so excited, I couldn't wait for it to come.

I was ready to start my new life as the deaf kid.

The aid arrived and to my delight, I was the star attraction in the class.

"Can I see it, Tyler? What does it feel like? Is it sore? What do I sound like to you when it's switched on?"

These were just some of the questions that I relished answering. I remember thinking I was really cool at the time; I was different, and I liked it. Everyone was looking at my ear because no one had ever seen a hearing aid before. It was all very new, very eventful.

At first, it felt like I had a microphone in my ear. I could hear things that I could never hear before. I didn't have to say 'pardon' anymore and could hear the teachers when they spoke. Everything just seemed that little bit louder and I was amazed. The aid itself was a transparent mould with a little tube going up to a battery pack which sat behind my ear. The pack was a burnt orange/reddish ugly colour. You could see it very plainly.

Sadly, after the novelty wore off and reality kicked in, wearing it felt awkward. It was too big and too noticeable. It made everything sound better which was great, but it came with lots of frustrations.

For the next few years, I was in constant physical pain, had endless ear infections, endured many trials of medication and faced numerous operations.

Not long after getting the hearing aid, my ear started becoming infected a lot which meant I couldn't wear the aid sometimes because it was too painful. I was often on medication for ear infections and it took a long time to find the right medication that would work. I had several operations during primary school for grommets to help me hear but they never worked. Due to all the infections, I got to the point where I was diagnosed with a permanent ear infection in my right ear, which was painful all the time.

My first memory of having the cannula in my arm and getting the anaesthetic through it. This was when I made the terrible discovery that anaesthetic was not my friend. I reacted very badly to it.

I dreaded every hospital visit after that, but, it would appear from no age, I wasn't going to suffer quietly.

I was managing to be quiet while the doctor spoke to my mum. Mum knew I was dreading the anaesthetic and the sickness that it would cause.

Understandably, due to the time I missed from school due to operations and the disruption to my concentration due to constant ear infections, I got behind in my learning and was referred to a psychologist.

It was at this point I was officially diagnosed with dyslexia and dyscalculia.

As a result of this my lovely Head Teacher, Mrs Sutton, arranged for me to get one to one support sessions with a wonderful teacher called Miss Doyle.

After my diagnosis, she came into primary school every week to teach me. I looked forward to her coming so much. My heart jumped when I saw her bobbed blonde head appear in the classroom. She always dressed very smart, in a black suit and carried a black handbag. She had the hugest smile and was so kind and interested in what I had to say. From day one I liked her, and I will never forget her.

Miss Doyle never said anything to suggest that I was behind the rest of my class in my work. She just brought me up to speed by teaching me the basic stuff in a fun and simple way. I remembered her lessons because she made them colourful and interesting. She used bright coloured beads to teach me maths. She gave me one of those magic sparkly pens that had lots of leads inside. They were new in the shops so none of the other kids had them. I loved removing the tips and putting them in the bottom and watching a new one pop out the top.

Miss Doyle ended all her sessions by playing Uno with me. She made learning fun.

I don't have one single bad memory of primary school. In a school of such a small population I was the only child with a disability.

So, yes, I was different to my classmates, but I was fully accepted and loved by all of them.

I know for sure that it's down to the examples set by Miss Sutton and Miss Doyle that I was never bullied there.

3. The Silent Treatment

No one understands how exhausting it is to read lips – I wish
they could live one day being deaf like me.

– Unknown

I was so excited starting high school. I expected it to be as fun
as primary school… full of lovely students and supportive
teachers but just on a larger scale.

It took only one day to dash my expectations.

I will always remember the first time I was called names.
I was on the bus on the way home during my first week.

As usual, my ear was sore, and I was keen to get home. I
looked around the bus at all the people and my heart sank. I
was so used to a tiny school and class at primary school.

Suddenly I heard a familiar boy's voice.

It was a quiet guy that I'd gone to primary school with,
shouting, "Doesn't she look like Shrek?"

Behind his mocking finger were a sea of faces, all looking
at me. Some nodding, some pointing but all laughing with
their hands up over their mouths.

That was the start of it… the name calling from teatime
that evening on that bus, all the way through high school, I
was called names.

I tried not to show that I was upset when they called me
names, but of course I was. Every time they called me a name,
my heart hurt more than even the searing pain in my ear.

Just like I had been in primary school, I was very open about my disabilities and the hearing aid was there for all the world to see but instead of accepting and loving me; teachers and pupils alike mocked and rejected me.

What was particularly hurtful was that a whole string of these names had nothing to do with my disability. They were purely because of what I looked like.

During my high school years, my mum used to get so frustrated at how much I scrutinised myself, trying to understand why people didn't want to be my friend. Thankfully, regardless of how nasty other people were about my looks, I never once wanted to change myself to be like them. I simply wanted to understand why they didn't like me. I was also very aware I was a country girl through and through. I often came to school looking like I had been dragged through a bush backwards. I didn't care about that either. I had no desire to straighten my hair, or have perfect nails or make up. That just wasn't me! I accepted everyone for who they were and what they look like.

My mum used to say to me just go to school tomorrow and come home and that's one more day out of the way. I remember sitting looking at the clock so many times and thinking there's just one more hour left of school and then I can go home.

Custard ear was another favourite insult for a long time in high school. This was particularly nasty because it came from the fact that I had an infected ear. Calling me this was like pouring salt on the wound. I was already in terrible physical pain all the time, which they could undoubtedly see. Yet, they decided to cause me mental pain by firing their poisoned verbal arrows right into my painful ears.

I used to dread taking the cotton wool out of my ear because I knew the nasty comments would start. Kids would ask me stupid things like why I had chewing gum in my ear. Some used to stand right in front of my face and mimic me, act like a deaf person and think this was funny.

Others used to creep up behind me and yell 'boo' in my ear then, in a whisper, ask me if I could hear them, if I was still deaf or was it all a lie. They accused me of faking it all the time.

Kids started picking on me outside of my school. One day, there was a crowd of boys drinking cider in the park near my house and they started saying horrible things and threw cider over me. My mum was raging and went and found them boys and threw water over them.

Even new kids from other year group started calling me Shrek. It was ridiculous. I didn't know them, and they certainly didn't know me. Obviously, word had spread about what the bullies were calling me, and they were copying the older kids to try to be cool.

No matter how much evidence teachers or pupils at high school got of my tormented school life, they were incapable of showing empathy or compassion.

I didn't have many people by my side during this difficult time, only when I got home and closed the door on my traumatic school life.

I am not sure if it would have been easier had I grown up in the town. I suppose potentially I would have been more streetwise. Maybe if I had been around more people I might have grown a thicker skin. Who knows?

The teachers knew I was being consistently bullied and did nothing.

It would appear some teachers weren't even made aware of my disability; they had to find out for themselves. I remember my hearing aid was whistling one day in class because it was losing battery charge and one of my teachers thought it was a phone and was going to confiscate it. I had to use disposable batteries and I was trying to fix it at the time. I had to explain to him that it was my hearing aid and I needed it to hear! Of course, he didn't apologise; teachers don't apologise for things like that.

There was also a teacher who flippantly commented on how loud I was by saying I was like a foghorn. From then on, that became yet another name I got called regularly.

I know he didn't mean any harm by it, but it just shows how horrible names can stick.

My mum was really cross about this and tried to speak with this teacher on several occasions, but he refused to see her.

Despite being officially diagnosed at primary school as being partially deaf and having dyslexia and dyscalculia, I was offered no support whatsoever at high school. I knew my school had a pastoral support and special needs team and yet they kept telling my mum they didn't have the resources to help me.

The only action they ever took was moving me to another class after nine months, but this did no good whatsoever.

If anything, I think they viewed me as a difficult jigsaw piece that just didn't fit. Rather than get me a support assistant like other people, they threw me into the same category as the difficult, unruly children that didn't want to learn, caused trouble all the time and were unlikely to get anywhere in life.

And yet, even the unruliest kids received some degree of support. They were taken out of the classroom to give them breathing space to calm down, or put in an exam room of their own and given extra time to improve their concentration and performance. I was never given any of this and yet, unlike them, I never caused trouble and I desperately wanted to learn. It felt like, because my disability wasn't obvious, I wasn't entitled to anyone fighting my corner or making sure the bullies were given suspension or report cards as punishment.

With no support, I ended up in the lowest sets for all my subjects. I was behind in my work because they had put me in a box and left me there. When I went to my teachers to tell them I was being bullied, they just shrugged it off. When I sat in class just staring into space because I didn't understand, my work my teachers just walked past and left me to it.

I was constantly coming home in tears. My mum and I were continuously going to the teacher looking for support.

I didn't care about looking like a tell-tale; I just wanted the torment to stop.

Sadly, I think it got to the stage where they simply didn't want to deal with us anymore.

My mum used to threaten to go to the papers with our story. When she did this, they panicked, met with her and promised her the world. They never kept their promises though.

I would have liked a support assistant in certain classes. I absolutely believe I should have had one in Maths and English. As for the rest, they were optional studies, and I didn't struggle in those because I had chosen them, and they were fun.

As far as friends were concerned, I didn't have many in high school. Some people would talk to me, but they would all succumb to peer pressure and join the bullies eventually.

If you can't beat 'em, join 'em. Isn't that what they say?

There were no friends that had my back or stuck up for me so there were times I just went off on my own breaks lunchtimes.

It got to the stage where our pleas were falling on deaf ears. For so long my mum's advice had been to be nice and walk away from the bullies. Then eventually she told me to say something back. I was never ever told to fight until one day my mum looked me right in the eye and said, if anyone hits you, you hit them back.

For a long time, I still didn't have it in me until one particular day... I saw red... and I fought back.

There was a girl who had been giving me grief and calling me names for years. She was someone who I considered a friend when I started high school that had turned against me and bullied me. It started with name calling but one day we had an argument about how I looked, and, whatever came over me, I retaliated by commenting on how she looked. Everyone who heard it was so shocked because I had never done this before. Of course, a whole crowd gathered and began to get quite rowdy because they were keen for the whole thing to turn into a big argument or a fight.

The bell rang for the next class, so I just got up and left. On my way to the next class, I saw the same girl and one of her friends holding the doors open for everyone but as I walked towards them, she jumped in front of me and we started arguing. As I pushed past her, she hit me from behind and when I turned round, she hit me again in my face.

At that point, an intense heat started to move up my body and I lifted the carrier bag with my PE stuff in it and swung it right into her face.

Then I started punching her. I was doing feeble little kangaroo punches, but I didn't care. I swung and made contact with her face again and again and again! I knew my swing and blow was improving every time and it felt good.

I couldn't stop; everything was a blur, but I could sense our whole year group had gathered around us and were shouting. My eyes focused for a moment and I could see that the girl was shocked. I was satisfied; it was time she got a shock!

I was mid punch when the teacher pulled me away. Through angry, yet relieved tears, I screamed at her that I'd been bullied for years and that she and the whole school knew it but had done nothing about it.

My teacher's expression said it all. She wasn't interested in my motives or my tears.

I took a long deep breath as I walked away, determined to stop crying.

A while later, I was in the staffroom when the same teacher stormed over towards me with the girl I was fighting with.

When she saw my face, she looked bewildered because I wasn't crying.

We had to go to our Head of Year for our punishment and while we were standing there waiting, this girl who had bullied me for five long years, wrapped her arms around me and said she was sorry, she was just having a crap lunchtime.

I was so thrown by what she said, I zoned out while she kept talking. She had a crap lunchtime? Try having a crap five years.

I didn't flinch or speak. I was simply not bothered by anything that was coming out of her mouth. I could see I'd bust her lip and her face was a bit red.

I vaguely heard the Head of Year ask her if she needed to go to first aid.

We had to be in isolation the following day.

I went home that night and couldn't wait to tell my mum that I had finally stuck up for myself, although, as I got closer to my house, I knew something was wrong because my uncle and my grandparents were there. My excitement dwindled and anxiety took over. I went inside and when my mum sat me and my brother down for a chat, I knew that my news wasn't the only news in our family that day. My mum informed us she had cervical cancer and me and my brother, my uncles and saw my granny all burst into tears. That was the first time I ever saw my grandma cry. Of course, I missed isolation the next day because I stayed home with my mum who told me she was happy I had finally stuck up for myself. My mum told my Head of Year about her diagnosis and she assured my mum that she would inform all my teachers.

I returned to school two days later and none of my teachers knew about my mum's cancer diagnosis. I had to tell them myself, which was so hard because it was still so raw. I was crying in the corridor telling my form tutor when the girl I had fought with walked past and smirked at me. I knew she had no idea what was going on in my life.

As well as the constant emotional pain of bullying during high school, I was often in terrible physical pain. My medical condition involved a lot of neurological exploration and treatment, a lot of poking around inside my ears; upsetting my inner balance. Painkillers didn't help at all with my constant ear infections. Eventually I got tablets from the doctors to draw out the infection but before that I had to get my ear syringed. The discomfort from this was off the scale as it caused extreme dizziness and nausea too. The infected area was always the concha, a very difficult place to treat and I still have a lump there from where the infection built up every time. After a lot of trial and error, I got eardrops that helped. However, on a few occasions, when I used these eardrops, I got dizzy, lost my balance and fell over.

I also had many operations during my time at high school, the biggest of these was when I was about 13/14. The operation was to remove my mastoid bone; the bone that stops your finger going any further when you put it in your ear. The operation was intended to allow more air to get through my ear in the hope it would help reduce my repeated ear infections. My mum was waiting for a radical hysterectomy and radiotherapy for her cancer at the time. I remember it was a really bad winter and the hospital had to collaborate wards because there weren't enough nurses to cover two wards. When my stepdad told the nurses about my mum's health issues, instead of putting my mum on a camp bed beside my hospital bed, they put us in our own ward to make sure we would both be comfortable. I remember going up and down to the toilet all night being sick because the anaesthetic was wearing off.

I was poorly for a few days afterwards because of the anaesthetic. The healing process was extremely painful, too, because everything was getting tighter inside the ear.

Not long after my return to school after this surgery I was going home on the school bus when several people started calling me names and hitting me around the face with their knotted ties. I was in tears because after my recent operation, my ear was very sensitive and still healing. My face was red raw and because of the trauma to my ear it started to bleed. Once I got off the bus, I ran home. I was so upset and in a state of shock. I couldn't even tell my mum what had happened. When my mum saw my face and the blood, she rushed straight out the door. She knew who was behind this incident because I'd had previous incidents involving this particular older boy in school. My mum spoke to his mother, but she openly admitted that she couldn't control her son and just apologised for his behaviour. Then my mum saw the boy walking past our house and got hold of him by the scruff of his neck. She told him to stay away from me and never hurt me again. She rang the police and informed them of the long list of things he had done to me. The police went to his house, which they were quite used to doing, but as usual, his mother claimed she couldn't do anything but apologised for his behaviour. Many people believed she was afraid of her own son.

The day after the bus incident, the school was informed, and the boy was suspended. Of course, I got grief from the cool crowd because of this.

After five long traumatic years, the last day of high school finally dawned. I watched the clock for the very last time and I embraced my freedom, vowing never to return to that hellish place ever again.

4. Counselling and Confidantes

Kindness is the language which the deaf can hear and the
blind can see.

– Mark Twain

I decided to go to college in the next town to avoid bumping
into the bullies I went to high school with. I didn't want to
face those people ever again.

My first few weeks were difficult because I didn't feel like
I fitted in and I was in a new place quite far away from home.

It turns out I wasn't allowing myself to fit in.

I had been emotionally damaged by my experience in high
school and that made me behave very defensively and rudely.
I had a bad aura around me towards everyone because I was
expecting to be bullied and mocked. I was simply protecting
myself the only way I knew how.

Many people tried to welcome me, but I threw it back in
their faces with attitude. There was one particular guy who
came over to me and simply asked what level of study I was
in. Whether you were in Level One, Two or Three depended
on your grades at high school.

I was in Level One and immediately assumed this guy was
going to take the mick out of me because of that. I was really
cheeky to him and told him it was none of his business and he
just walked off. It turned out he was in level three but had
started college in Level One and worked his way up. He just
wanted to know if I was going to be in his class and was being

friendly. I had massive regrets about speaking to him so horribly when I realised he wasn't going to disrespect or make fun of me.

Thankfully, despite my moody, snappy response that guy never held it against me and kept being lovely to me.

Slowly, I began to let the defence barriers down, but it took support from great people and counselling sessions to get me there.

There was another guy who was a joker, a Jack the Lad.

He was all about the banter and at the time I simply didn't understand banter. I took everything people said to heart or saw it as an attack. It got to the stage with him that when he said something in banter, I responded really harshly. One day, he asked me what my problem was and tried to explain that he was just trying to have a laugh. We ended up in a really heated argument with the whole class standing round listening. The college tutor barged in and I ran out of the room and burst into tears. I was so overwhelmed with emotion and suddenly realised he hadn't done anything wrong.

In the end, my misunderstanding turned out to be a blessing because this argument led me into counselling after my college tutor referral.

When I and this guy got into a room together with the college tutors, I explained what I had been through in high school and they were so supportive. The sad truth was, I didn't know how to handle someone being genuinely nice to me because it had never happened to me before. I will never forget that day because it was the beginning of a genuine, proper friendship. I went to shake his hand and he just wrapped his arms around me and gave me a big hug. I was really shocked because no peer had ever treated me that well.

To be honest, I didn't want to go to counselling at first. I didn't know much about it and I certainly didn't think it would work.

Thank goodness, I did go because it kept me in college, which turned out to be one of the best experiences of my life. I felt like I was back at primary school because we were in such a small class and were all so close. There were about six or seven of us and then we were friends with others on different courses, too.

Between counselling and my supportive classmates, I thrived. Over time, not only did I speak to my college counsellor about what I'd been through, but my classmates also knew. Not only did they know, but the beautiful thing was they understood and were so supportive. If anything, they were nurturing towards me, including the guy who was all about the banter. Every time he said anything, he would put his arm around me as if to try to toughen me up in a brother like way. I knew that everyone was trying to look after me and protect me, which felt amazing.

During college I met a guy who was on a different level to me. We started going out and it was like any other young romance. We spent a lot of time together doing fun things and hanging out with other students.

I left college in this relationship and we both started looking for work with the intention of starting a life together. I got my first job as an apprentice where I worked in the cash office for a year.

I really enjoyed this and ended up helping some of my former high school bullies to fill in forms or give advise to them. They acted sheepish in front of me.

It felt very satisfying to be a professional working person sitting opposite these people who had tried to stunt my intellectual growth for years.

I felt confident in the knowledge that I could teach them a thing or two.

After this, I moved onto another department where I worked with many lovely people and befriended some. The work place were brilliant at hiring people with disabilities and from diverse backgrounds. They were also fantastic at providing and funding training courses about many different types of disabilities and trained people in how to work with people with disabilities and how to support them. These courses were open to everybody from every department.

Despite all their efforts, however, the workplace couldn't make people go on these courses or change their misconceptions and inform their uneducated minds. Unfortunately, people need to want to educate themselves about disability and I discovered, in the world of work especially, there are so many who don't think these courses are relevant to them.

One person I befriended was fully deaf and required a sign language interpreter while they worked.

Despite all training on offer, I noticed that people ignored them most of the day. I sat with them and we communicated the best we could using sign language or writing things down.

I don't know whether it's a lack of education, a lack of compassion, a lack of empathy or a lack of understanding, but there is no excuse for treating them the way some people did.

During my time there, I had a baby and during my maternity leave, I decided on a career change. I left my job and went back to college where I studied AAT. I informed the college of my disabilities; and so I was reassessed. Once again, I was diagnosed with dyslexia and dyscalculia. I am glad I got re-assessed because now I have a twenty-page diagnostic review that I can present to employers and even though a lot of it is medical jargon, I now better understand and appreciate my disabilities.

I found the AAT course enjoyable even though I wasn't as quick as my peers. It was an evening class so once the class was over at 9 pm, understandably, the tutors wanted to go home rather than stay and go over stuff with me.

I invested the extra time and effort it took and eventually, with a little struggle, I completed the course and got my qualification. If it's easy to get, it's not worth having.

Tyler, the young girl diagnosed with profound numerical difficulties, was on her way to being a bona fide accountant. How fantastic was that!

5. Bringing Others to Account

It's not about how long it takes you to get there it about getting there in the end.

– Tyler Casey

During my AAT course, I got my first job working in accountancy which was exactly where I wanted to be.

As always, I was open about my disability and told my employers and colleagues about the difficulties I faced in my AAT course and they seemed supportive.

During the job interview, I was told to finish my level 2 studies and that my employer would fund my Level 3 studies. I was delighted and I put my trust in them to honour their word.

Like any new job, I tried to fit in, progress in my work and enjoy the office environment, however, it wasn't long before I felt patronised and humiliated by the people I worked with. My mistakes were highlighted time and time again in front of everyone in the office. It felt like my colleagues didn't care that I was new in the industry and to my studies.

They didn't have the time or patience to explain how to do something, especially to a person with disabilities!

I knew I was different and that I worked in a different way, but I was ok with that. It was others that weren't. I knew I had difficulties that my team members didn't have but I was determined to overcome these difficulties and do as good a job as them.

Many things went wrong in work and it got to the stage where I felt I was being set up to fail.

On one occasion I had completed something called a bank reconciliation on a Monday, but when I logged into my office computer on Tuesday, my work had vanished.

I told a colleague that my work was gone but that I had definitely completed it. In the office in front of everyone they said I obviously hadn't done it because it wasn't there. People started gathering around my desk to have a look and I felt so humiliated. Another colleague actually said that I had ticked amounts to make it look like I'd done it. I was so frustrated and went to see if I could retrieve my filename from yesterday; I found it and I printed it out and took it to my manager. This was proof that I had done the work. I was in tears to my manager but they just said 'aww, Tyler, you're just new, you're just finding it hard to settle in. It will get better eventually. It's probably just an easy mistake.'

I felt so let down. They were trying to fob me off but I was convinced someone had deleted my work. My manager was having none of it, so I went for a walk and rang some of my family for support.

Another situation happened, with a colleague who had 15/20 years' experience in accountancy. I had booked annual leave and had one task left to complete. The colleague told me to go ahead on annual leave and they would complete the task for me. I knew they hadn't done it before, but I thought because they had so many more years' experience than me, they'd know what they were doing.

They assured me they did, and I believed them. They were a very knowledgeable and wise person, after all, so I had no reason to doubt them.

This was on a Friday, and I came back on Monday to about 60 angry emails from employees. Then a colleague came over to my desk. He said that the task I had completed Friday was wrong and he had to fix them when he was far too busy to do so. He was ranting and raving at me and I just sat in my chair gobsmacked. When I looked over at the person who had offered to help me, they turned to another colleague, and they left the office. I turned to the man who was giving me a mouthful and told him I didn't do the task but that our colleague did and insisted they knew what they was doing. To be fair to him he was shocked that this person could behave in the way that they did, but there were no repercussions for the person who did wrong.

Previously I had asked the same person in training why they did another task the way they did and they snapped at me, 'Tyler, I am only human and sometimes I make mistakes and thank you for making me share that with everybody!' From that moment on, I realised they didn't like admitting to making mistakes. The way I see it, everyone makes mistakes and should just own them.

By the end of my first year in this job, things had just gone from bad to worse. People said I shouldn't be working in finance and another told my manager I should be a receptionist instead of an accountant! Not that there's anything wrong with any job but why diminish my hard work to get my qualification in AAT. To this day, it bewilders me why my manager ever told me this.

In subsequent management meetings on zoom or on telephone, I got pulled up for various things. One was the tone of my emails to one woman in particular. I apologised for the emails, but I also stressed that emails could easily be misinterpreted. It made me laugh because the woman complaining about my tone was one of the most blunt and direct woman I'd ever met. Ironically, she was quite similar to me in that she wrote how she talked. When I heard that she was complaining, I was tempted to tell her how I felt when I read some of her short, abrupt emails.

It wasn't not long in work before it felt like I couldn't do right for doing wrong. Every time I had a meeting with my manager, I was thinking what's next? And I was finding it quite draining.

I had been working in the company for a year when I, my manager and the HR explored colleges and I chose the one I wished to study my Level 3 at.

The college started sending me enrolment forms and when I told my manager, they told me they'd speak to HR. I continued filling in the forms as normal and sent them to the college. A week later, HR and my manager had a meeting with me and advised me they wouldn't be paying for my level 3, after all.

I was absolutely gutted. They told me I wasn't as progressed as they'd like me to be. I tried to explain myself, but it felt like they weren't listening.

I couldn't believe what I was hearing. Not progressing? I knew I'd made mistakes, but who doesn't? I mean there had been many times in work when other people made a mistake and blamed it on me because I was an easy target. These people with 15/20 years' experience on me just didn't want to admit they had made a mistake, so it was easier to blame someone like me who had only been in the role for a year. The difference between me and most of my colleagues was that I was prepared to hold my hands up when I made mistakes.

This notion that I wasn't progressing was so insulting. I was desperate to progress, but they wouldn't let me. I had asked repeatedly to be shown how to do certain tasks to help me progress but got nowhere. I reminded my manager of this. I told them that I often took on other people's job roles and tasks when asked. I quizzed him on why people didn't mind giving me work when it helped them but when I asked for work to help me progress, they said no sorry you can't do that. I was constantly appealing to my team and management to give me something that I would actually like to learn.

They ended up saying they would maybe put me through my studies next year. They also waffled on about the current climate and the impact it had had on work performance across the whole country. If anything, that offended me! I felt like they were insulting my intelligence and I was adamant I wasn't falling for that, as I was aware the company was thriving.

As if this wasn't bad enough, they then advised me to go to occupational health and access to work to see if I was fit to work!

Talk about feeling completely floored! That was the icing on the cake and I was devastated. I had worked from 14 years old. Of course I was fit for work. It felt like they thought I couldn't be an accountant because of my disabilities.

I wasn't surprised when occupational health advised me there was nothing they could do because I was fit and healthy.

I explained how the working environment was making me feel and the lady sympathised with me.

Access to Work were shocked I had been referred to them because that was a service for people who struggled to get into work and to give people supportive aids in work, whereas I'd worked for years without needing any aids.

Despite acknowledging this, my Access to Work advisor went on to inform my employers what aids were available for someone with my disabilities. I told them I didn't want the equipment because I was well aware of my struggles. Despite what I said, my employers went ahead and bought the aids. After this, I was bombarded with loads of emails for training courses on my own disability and how to deal with it in the workplace!

As much as I appreciated my employer offering me to equipment, I didn't feel I needed it because the aids simply weren't of any specific assistance to my work in accountancy.

At this point, I was sent on a raft of training courses while my colleagues were only asked to do one. The company paid for the sessions so, out of respect and gratitude, I joined them, but they were waste of time. My first training session was a three hour tutorial on how to use aid software which I was unable to use on the computer software the company had. These training sessions went on for weeks. Part of it was informative, however, I feel it was informing the wrong person. I feel like my team members should have been there.

We were put on a team training session that my colleagues weren't one bit happy about. When my manager explained during a conference call that we were all going to undergo disability awareness training, one woman sighed and said in a horrible tone that she knew it must have something to do with me. It was obvious she didn't like me, and she couldn't be bothered trying to understand my disability. I just shook my head at the other end of the phone when she spoke in that tone because her attitude and many others who shared this attitude were the reason why I felt the way I did.

Ironically, I ended up being put on two training sessions a month – my colleagues only one. I didn't need to know more about my disability because I was the one living through it, understand that?

I have been on so many training courses now, I've lost track. I feel frustrated because I am being expected to change how I work in order to suit everyone else.

I informed the trainer that all these courses weren't going to change how I was or how I worked. I insisted it was my colleagues that needed to change their mind-set and their treatment of people with disabilities.

After many discussions with a number of managers, I got to the stage in work where I felt I had no choice but to file a grievance against the treatment I had faced. My managers had been advising me to for some time. When I started this process, I was horrified to discover that they don't have a single policy in place about discrimination towards people with disabilities.

Prior to my grievance being submitted, I had to attend one to ones weekly with management while my colleagues had fortnightly meetings.

I questioned why I had to have weekly meetings because it suggested to me there were more problems with me, rather than other people. I was told I was complaining about the wrong thing and I should be more appreciative of the time my manager gives me.

I have been in touch with someone who left the same company due to quite similar circumstances. They were off sick due to mental health issues and they told me they used to pile work and pressure onto them. Even the manager used to give some of their own workload as extra work.

This was the first accountancy environment I had ever worked in and up until this person shared their experience, I believed this was how accounting industries were. I thought I just had to put up and shut up because I wanted to be in this industry. The person told me it was the worst company they'd ever worked for and other companies that they have worked for since were shocked at what this company had put their staff through. There was also such a high staff turn-around, which isn't a good sign.

They were still trying to tell me that finance isn't for me and I get so frustrated, I just want to scream at them, Who do you think you're talking to? You can't tell someone what their worth is and what their worth isn't. You can't disrespect someone like that.

Recently, my manager told me they just wanted me to be 100%. I told them that not one member of the team was 100%.

I reminded them once again, like a broken record, that the only reason I appeared less than perfect was that, unlike the others, I was prepared to put my hands up and admit when I'd made a mistake.

I feel that all that the company did was put me through disrespect and humiliation. My mistakes were highlighted where others' weren't. I have been disciplined and others haven't.

I felt like I was being told I wasn't good enough all the time. Nobody should have to feel like that day in, day out.

Weirdly though, being so consistently ridiculed is part of the reason why I stuck there for so long. I was applying for other jobs but I wasn't going to allow them to get the better of me and I wasn't going to let them bully me out the door.

My experience over the last few years has proven to me that there is no end to discrimination. It doesn't end at high school. For a long time, I foolishly believed I had left the heartache of high school behind me, but then I went into the workplace and experienced the same pain and worse.

I feel extremely passionate and infuriated about this now because I have a daughter and I found out when I got in touch with a lawyer about my grievance that this could have had a devastating impact on my family. I could have been written off as unfit to work. I knew in my heart of hearts I would never have been declared unfit to work, but I am more than aware that this is a very likely outcome for people with disabilities.

I have a child, I live in a lovely area, I have a lovely home and to think my daughters and my life could have come crashing down around us devastates me. I want the best for my child, and I will try my hardest to give my child the best life. No one will make my choices for me and they certainly won't make my daughter's choices.

My manager was disappointed by Occupational Health's response. They said that they expected more of an answer and asked me how they were supposed to know what was wrong with me? They asked me how they were supposed to know what my disabilities were and how they could help me.

I longed to say, listen to me and I can tell you how you can help me! But they didn't want to. So many times, I have rehearsed what I would like to say to them but probably never will.

I feel like I am being told what I need by people who never listen to me.

I've had several conversations with several managers and HR on the phone. I've been in tears several times but never once has anybody ever shown any sort of empathy or compassion; there isn't even one recording or a sheet of notes from the meetings I've left in tears.

Never once did anyone take my mental health into consideration and suggest they terminate the meeting so that I could calm down and take time to process things in a healthy way.

A manager once said in a meeting that they didn't think finance was for me. My response was this, 'Thank you for your opinion but I've been in finance since I was 18 years old and with or without your support or anybody else's, I will be an accountant!

We left the meeting at that.

I am well aware that there are very few people working in accounting and finance that have a disability. People in these jobs tend to be crazy smart; they eat, sleep, repeat finance.

They are not like me in so many ways.

One main difference between us is that they believe that somebody who has a disability can't work in finance whereas I know that they can, and I can prove it.

It's primarily all the things I've gone through in work that has made me want to write this book. I want to make sure I and others don't have to go through this torture again in my working life.

I am only young and I won't retire till I'm 70. So I have plenty of time to find and settle in a healthy and happy working environment where I can excel in the job I know I was born to do.

Today, in 2023, I honestly feel like, despite all the aids, the courses, and the software available, the attitudinal workings of the human mind towards people with disabilities has been at a standstill since Victorian times.

My hope, by telling my story, is to change as many attitudes as I can.

6. Dreams and Determination

In general terms, my dream is to be a hugely successful advocate for change. By the time my daughter is 20, I want to have been instrumental in putting more people with disabilities in managerial roles. I also want to have had a part to play in ensuring more children at primary and high school age learn Makaton within the school and undergo disability training.

Very few good accessible courses exist in our schools and workplaces, so I'd like to encourage more training courses to be available and for it to be mandatory for those working with disabled people to attend.

I see myself as an advocate for any disabled person out there who feels like they're not good enough for society or they are unable to do what they want to do in society because of misconceptions.

To deny people an integrated work or school environment, as far as I am concerned, is unforgivable.

It frustrates me so much that disabled people are constantly having to change their way of working to accommodate those around them like we don't have enough pressures on us trying to fit in with society anyway. We were born with these difficulties and we can't help it.

I think, rather than send us on a million training courses, more of society should go to training on how to work with us.

I would be delighted if a broadcaster or a celebrity wanted to endorse my book. Like Marcus Rashford, the England footballer who wrote a children's book recently. Marcus has also launched a book club to get disadvantaged children reading more. I am not a football fan, but I am a personal fan of his because he is a fantastic advocate for change in underprivileged communities. He is very open and honest about his own childhood and financial struggles.

He has changed the UK for many kids during lockdown by lobbying the government to provide meals to families struggling to put food on the table.

I would love to challenge the government to make changes to transform the UK into a more welcoming and nurturing place for disabled people. I feel Makaton should be included as part of the curriculum in all schools. The government and educational authorities are so keen that every student learn a second language and yet the deaf community in this country learn Makaton, why can't Makaton be everyone's second language? I feel like we should be learning our own mother tongue in all the ways that it exists before learning another language. It's so important to make people with disabilities feel included in a country that they have been born and raised in and a country that is their home. In the future, a day should come when no one is singled out or put in a corner out of the way like I and other have been.

Another personal dream is that this book might feature on reading lists in schools, colleges and workplaces. It is books like this that can go a long way in helping people understand that disability is merely one part of a person, it does not define them.

I take great inspiration in my young life from another successful young woman who is crating tidal waves of respect in the public eye just now. A deaf woman who is shining the light on what it is like to be deaf in a very noisy and busy world.

This girl is Rose Ayling Ellis, the Eastender's actor who took the Strictly Come Dancing stage by storm. Rose is a prime example of succeeding against the odds. Each week she danced beautifully to the beat of music that she couldn't hear. She performs impeccably. As I watched her, I think about my journey against the odds in the competitive world of accountancy despite being diagnosed with dyscalculia.

If this isn't testament to how there are many other ways to communicate other than direct speech, I don't know what is. As I watch Rose dance by feeling the vibrations on the floor, I think about my journey against the odds through the world of accountancy with dyscalculia and dyslexia creating many obstacles along the way.

Unlike Rose, I don't have a captive TV audience of millions, nor a fan-base of millions like Marcus Rashford. What I do have, however, is one of the most powerful means of communication known to man – the written word. May the words of my story dance into the hearts of many for years and years to come, because unlike the spoken word that disappears once said, the written word is lasting. Long after I am gone from this earth, my story will live on in the hearts of the wonderful people who took the time to read it.

My journey has barely begun, and yet I am so excited for what's ahead. Who knows? Maybe there will be another book!

Wherever you are on your journey and whether travelling it with a disability or not, there will be bumps in the road.

I dream that my story of climbing over many bumps on this earth will inspire you to leap over yours.

For now, as you keep journeying, here are a few challenges for YOU to think about as you move forward, in a sometimes, deaf and alien world...

Pick one small thing to achieve every week and go for it.

Remind yourself every morning that the world wouldn't be complete without you in it. Then tell yourself why.

Picture someone who has always had your back and imagine the world full of people like that.

When people mock you, lift your head, look at your phone, say is that the time? Then walk away, sending the message that your time is too precious to bother with them.

Every single time you succeed at anything, write it down, pin it on your fridge and reward yourself.

So, to anyone who has related to this book, firstly thank you for reading it. Secondly, never give up, raise your voice so it's heard and if you want something, go and get it; define your own odds. And always remember:

'It's not how long it takes you to get there – it's about getting there in the end'

"Never give up, raise your voice, so it's heard and if you want something, go and get it. Define your own odds." And always remember: "It's not how long it takes you to get there – it's about getting there in the end!"

Tyler's story is one of strength and resilience. Diagnosed at a young age with dyscalculia, dyslexia and being hard of hearing, she faced bullies and unsupportive learning environments. When she started work, despite all her achievements, people continued to try and bring her down. However, Tyler has come through the other side stronger than ever. Whatever life throws at her, she prevails, and her story will make you think twice about putting her, or anyone else in a box.